5 -

W9-ANX-064

THE WISDOM OF
ZEN

Compiled by Marc de Smedt
Calligraphy and sumi-e by Master Taisen Deshimaru

Abbeville Press   Publishers
New York   London   Paris

Cover illustration and vignettes by Danielle Siegelbaum

For the English-language edition
RESEARCH, TRANSLATION FROM THE FRENCH, AND BIBLIOGRAPHY:
John O'Toole
EDITOR: Jacqueline Decter
TYPOGRAPHIC DESIGN: Virginia Pope
PRODUCTION EDITOR: Owen Dugan

For the original edition
SERIES EDITORS: Marc de Smedt and Michel Piquemal

First edition
10 9 8 7 6 5 4 3 2 1

Library of Congress Cataloging-in-Publication Data

Paroles zen. English.
The wisdom of Zen/compiled by Marc de Smedt; calligraphy by
Taisen Deshimaru.
p. cm.
Includes bibliographical references.
ISBN 0-7892-0240-9
1. Zen Buddhism. I. Smedt, Marc de, 1946–   . II. Title.
BQ9266.P3713 1996
294.3'927—dc20

                                        96–21418

The Japanese word *Zen* means "meditation." It defines a school of Buddhism in Japan that emphasizes the practice of seated meditation based on the Buddha's own experience.

The annals tell of how twenty-five hundred years ago the Buddha, while walking near a field, suddenly asked a peasant to cut him an armful of long, pliant grass called *sala* in order to bundle the stalks into a round cushion on which to meditate. Elsewhere it is said that on entering the peace and quiet of a forest he would sometimes choose a stone or gather fallen leaves to make a support that would allow him to remain firmly seated in the posture he had adopted from among so many in the yoga exercises of enlightenment.

Actually, the posture the Buddha had taken up was the

basic *raja yoga* (royal yoga), which entails sitting in the lotus or half-lotus position, that is, with one's legs either completely or half crossed. The cushion that he added to the practice of this posture was not for comfort alone. It allows one to stretch out the spine better by arching it naturally and to adopt a more stable position by anchoring the knees firmly on the ground. Seated in this manner, practitioners must then place the left hand, open and palm up, in the right, with the thumbs held horizontally and their tips touching (see photograph on page 48), and concentrate their attention on a deeply exhaled breath that descends below the navel, penetrating the abdomen. At the same time, on the level of consciousness, one simply watches thought-images stream by, allowing them to pass continuously, like clouds in the sky. In this way we become observers of our own mental universe, now seeing ourselves moving about, fretting, dreaming, and imagining. Gradually this whirlwind subsides within us, and the roiling torrent turns into a peaceful river that allows us to discover an inner silence and a genuine contact with reality. This reality is no longer fantasized but is seen with a clear vision, a vision freed of the dross that had cluttered it up.

This simple posture was the basis then of the Buddha's entire instruction. He passed it on to his followers who, generation after generation, spread it to the whole of the Indian subcontinent and Southeast Asia. In the sixth century A.D. a monk from the island of Sri Lanka, Bodhidharma, arrived in southern China. There, after many long years of meditation in a cave, he founded the famous Shao-Lin monastery. His teachings were later transmitted throughout China under the name of Ch'an Buddhism.

It was not until the twelfth century that another monk, Dogen, traveled from Japan to China and there, in a monastery, was initiated into the practice of this type of meditation. He then returned to his native island to impart what he had learned to others. It was at this time that the expression *zen* came into use to define both the posture (*zazen: za*, "seated"; *zen*, "meditation") and the school of philosophy that took shape around it.

The principles conveyed by this teaching in a rather abrupt, even harsh, language, espouse psycho-philosophical concepts that come down to a single formula: letting go. We are constantly involved with the world, forever wanting to grasp or obtain something; Buddhism also points out that we are hungry spirits, true vultures of thought. This behavior leads us to a kind of ordinary madness whose outcome is seen in human civilization. To combat the perverse effects of this attitude, we need to learn detachment. This does not mean abandoning everything. To know how to be detached is an inner attitude, an outlook on a given situation, a distance one needs to maintain with respect to oneself, an ethics to be applied in living one's life. As the Zen master Taisen Deshimaru said, it is useless to wish to retreat to a cave deep in the heart of a mountain in order to learn to let go. Wherever the meditative posture is practiced, it serves in effect as that mountain cave.

The aim of this practice is to find inner peace and the original scope of our mind, of our entire being, because finding peace within ourselves enables us to create peace around us. It is certainly difficult to solve the world's problems before solving one's own. How are we to succeed in leading a just existence? How are we to create a pure energy?

Zen strives to provide answers to these questions, too. It is, I think, a possible path towards wisdom for each of us, regardless of our religion or lack of one, a practice of enlightenment that is universal enough to be useful to us both in this day and age and in the millennium to come.

Whether in the form of tales, historic dialogues between masters and their students, traditional teachings, or famous *koans* (enigmatic and paradoxical statements that are intended to spark enlightenment), the passages presented in this volume bear witness to that very spirit.

Marc de Smedt

Just as you see yourself in a mirror,

form and reflection look at each other.

You are not the reflection

yet the reflection is you.

Master Tosan
Hokyo Zan Mai
(The Samadhi of the Mirror of the Treasure)

A Brace of Sparrows on the Budding Branch of a Plum Tree

No pine has two colors, old and new.

Koan

Cedar Forest

In darkness light exists, do not look with a dark view.

In light darkness exists, do not look with a luminous view.

Light and darkness create an opposition, yet depend on each other just as the step taken by the right leg depends on the step taken by the left.

Master Sekito
San Do Kai

Chestnuts, Sweet Savor in a Prickly Husk

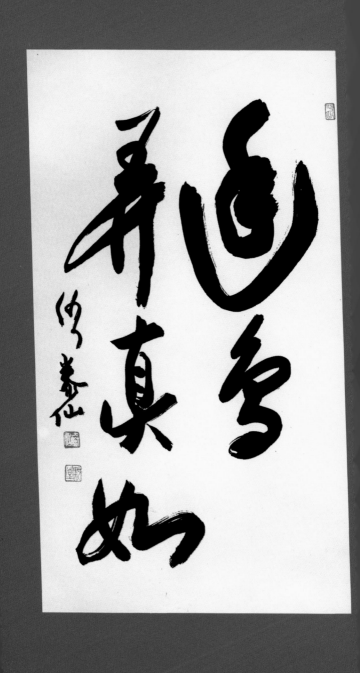

Walking is Zen, sitting is Zen.

Whether talking or remaining silent, whether moving or standing quiet, the Essence itself is ever at ease.

Even when greeted with swords and spears it never loses its quiet way.

So with poisonous drugs, they fail to perturb its serenity.

Master Daishi
Song of Enlightenment

The Mysterious Bird at Play

Man looks at the flower,

the flower smiles.

Koan

Wild Chrysanthemum

What was your face

before the birth of your parents?

Koan

Distant Landscape of a Mountain Village in the Morning Mist

M aster Ummon said: "About the fifteen days past I do not ask you. But about the fifteen days to come, say something." Nobody answered. Ummon himself said, "Every day is a good day."

In a small temple lost in the mountains four monks were practicing zazen. The four decided to observe seven days of silence.

On the first day all were silent. Their meditation had begun auspiciously, but when night came and the oil lamps were growing dim one of the pupils could not help exclaiming to a servant: "Fix those lamps."

The second pupil was surprised to hear the first one talk: "We are not supposed to say a word."

"You two are stupid. Why did you talk?" asked the third.

"I am the only one who has not talked," concluded the fourth pupil.

P ure water penetrates the depths of the earth. Thus, when a fish swims in that water, it has the freedom of the true fish.

The sky is vast and transparent to the limits of the cosmos. Thus, when a bird flies in the sky, it has the freedom of the true bird.

Master Dogen
Zazen Shin
(The Spirit of Zazen)

There once was a king who was determined to own a champion fighting cock, and he asked one of his subjects to train one for him. The man began by teaching the cock all the techniques of combat.

After ten days the king asked, "Can I organize a fight for this cock?"

The trainer said, "Certainly not! He's strong enough, yes; but his strength is empty, hot air; he wants to fight all the time, he's overexcited, he has no endurance."

Ten days later the king again asked the trainer, "Now can I organize a fight?"

"No, no! Not yet. He's still too fierce, he's still looking for a fight all the time. Whenever he hears another rooster crowing, even in the next village, he flies into a rage and wants to fight."

Another ten days of training, and the king made his request a third time. "Now is it possible?"

Maku, the Horse of Emptiness

The trainer replied, "Well, he no longer flies into a passion now, he remains calm when he hears another cock crowing. His posture is good, and  he has a lot of power in reserve. He has stopped losing his temper all the time. Looking at him, you aren't even aware of his energy and strength."

"So we can go ahead with the fight?" asked the king.

The trainer said, "Maybe."

So a great many fighting cocks were assembled and the tournament began. But no bird would come anywhere near that one. They all ran away terrified; and he never needed to fight.

The fighting cock had become a cock of wood. He had gone beyond his technical training. He possessed enormous energy but it was all inside, he never showed it. That way, his power stayed within himself, and the others had no choice but to bow before his tranquil assurance and undisplayed strength.

Master Taisen Deshimaru
The Zen Way to the Martial Arts

一月輪掛
一輪燈

The mind's bright moonglow,

pure, unsullied, spotless,

breaks the waves that rush upon the shore

and flood it with light.

Master Deshimaru

The Moon as a Circle of Fire

Ours is the exhaling of the entire universe.

Ours is the inhaling of the entire universe.

Thus we accomplish at every moment

the great limitless work.

To possess that spirit is to clear away

unhappiness and create absolute happiness.

Master Kodo Sawaki

Eagle on a Mountain Peak
"To Be Practicing Zazen Alone on the Great Mountain"

A free mind,

a free universe.

Koan

A Circle, Image of the Universe

Nan-in, a Japanese master during the Meiji era (1868–1912), received a university professor who came to inquire about Zen.

Nan-in served tea. He poured his visitor's cup full, and then kept on pouring.

The professor watched the overflow until he no longer could restrain himself. "It is overfull. No more will go in!"

"Like this cup," Nan-in said, "you are full of your own opinions and speculations. How can I show you Zen unless you first empty your cup?"

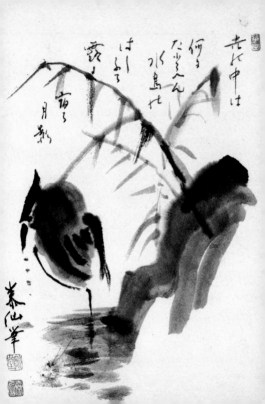

Hogen, a Chinese Zen master, lived alone in a small temple in the country. One day four traveling monks appeared and asked if they might make a fire in his yard to warm themselves.

While they were building the fire, Hogen heard them arguing about subjectivity and objectivity. He joined them and said, "There is a big stone. Do you consider it to be inside or outside your mind?"

One of the monks replied, "From the Buddhist viewpoint everything is an objectification of mind, so I would say that the stone is inside my mind."

"Your head must feel very heavy," observed Hogen, "if you are carrying around a stone like that in your mind."

A Heron Standing in Water beneath Reeds
"To What Can We Compare Our Life?
The Reflection of the Moon in a Drop of Dew Falling from the Beak of a Bird."

Some claim to correct evil and lead to good. But this is only a passing desire.

Winning and losing is the ignorance that makes one believe in personality and the self.

I would like to be a mind beyond the dust.

Blue sky and white moon.

The wind sends us pure air.

Master Ikkyu
Crazy Clouds

Old Bronze Incense Burner

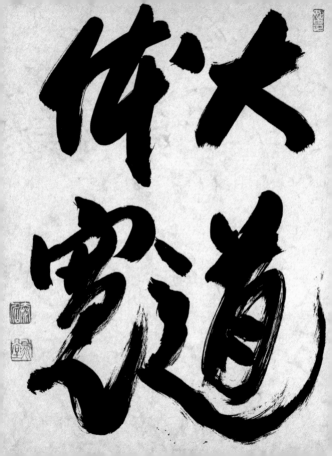

The twentieth patriarch had said:

"I do not seek the way,
    and I do not do the opposite either.

I do not prostrate myself before the Buddha,
    but I do not despise him either.

I do not remain seated [meditating] for very long,
    but I am not mindless either.

I do not limit myself to a single meal,
    but I do not stuff myself either.

I am not satisfied with everything,
    but I am not covetous.

When the heart is stripped of all desire,
    that is the Way."

The Great Way Is Generous
So It Is neither Difficult nor Easy

能隨

境滅

A monk asked Joshu why Bodhidharma came to China.

Joshu said, "An oak tree in the garden."

Mumon's comment:

Words cannot describe everything.

The heart's message cannot be delivered in words.

If one receives words literally, he will be lost,

If he tries to explain with words, he will not attain enlightenment in this life.

The Subject Disappears by Following the Object

The Perfect Way knows no difficulties

Except that it refuses to make preferences;

Only when freed from hate and love,

It reveals itself fully and without disguise.

Master Sosan
Shinjin-no-Mei
(On Believing in Mind)

The Round Moon Rises above a Mountain Peak

The blue mountain bordering the sea does not move, but the mind of the bird over the waves breaks free and follows the course of the river.

Master Daishi

Small Bird on a Stone Covered with Moss

All of the calligraphy and sumi-e (India ink wash drawings) illustrating this volume are the work of Master Taisen Deshimaru (1914–1982), a Zen master who was an inspiration in the spread of the spirit of Zen and the practice of Zen meditation throughout Europe during his fifteen years of teaching there.

Selected Bibliography

Claremon, Neil. *Zen in Motion: Lessons from a Master Archer on Breath, Posture, and the Path of Intuition.* Rochester, Vt.: Inner Traditions International, 1990.

Deshimaru, Taisen. *Questions to a Zen Master.* New York: Dutton, 1985.

———. *The Ring of the Way: Testament of a Zen Master.* New York: Dutton, 1987.

———. *The Zen Way to the Martial Arts.* New York: Dutton, 1982.

Hoffmann, Yoel. *The Sound of One Hand: 281 Zen Koans with Answers.* New York: Basic Books, 1975. (A bracing compilation and exposition of this most enigmatic form of expression on the path to enlightenment.)

Ikemoto, Takashi, and Lucien Stryk. *Zen: Poems, Prayers, Sermons, Anecdotes, Interviews.* Athens, Oh.: Swallow Press, 1981. (A good anthology of Zen writings.)

———. *Zen Poetry: Let the Spring Breeze Enter.* New York: Grove Press, 1995. (This anthology of Zen poetry translated from the Japanese and the Chinese is also available from Penguin under the title *The Penguin Book of Zen Poetry.*)

Reps, Paul. *Zen Flesh, Zen Bones: A Collection of Zen and Pre-Zen Writings.* New York: Anchor Books, 1961 (reissued by Doubleday, 1989).

Shigematsu, Soiku. *A Zen Forest: Sayings of the Masters.* New York: Weatherhill, 1981.

Stevens, John. *Three Zen Masters: Ikkyū, Hakuin, Ryōkan.* New York: Kodansha International, 1993.

Suzuki, D. T. *An Introduction to Zen Buddhism.* New York: Grove Press, 1964 (paperback reprint).

———. *Essays in Zen Buddhism, First Series.* New York: Grove Press, 1961 (paperback reprint of the 1949 edition).

———. *Manual of Zen Buddhism.* London: Rider, 1983.

Watson, Burton. *Ryōkan: Zen Monk-Poet of Japan.* New York: Columbia University Press, 1977.

Wu, John C. H. *The Golden Age of Zen.* New York: Image Book, 1996 (reprint of a 1967 edition).